LITERATURE & LANGUAGE DEPT.
CHICAGO PUBLIC LIBRARY
400 SOUTH STATE STREET
CHICAGO, IL 60605

scratching for something

scratching for something

kim white

```
PS 3573 .H4737 S38 1998
White, Kim, 1967-
Scratching for something
```

A Quarto Book

Copyright © 1998 by Kim White.
All rights reserved

a Quarto book
Columbia University Creative Writing Center
Columbia University offers writing courses for degree and nondegree candidates.
For information, contact the Creative Writing Center
Mail Code 4108, Lewisohn Hall, Columbia University, New York, NY 10027
email: writingprogram@columbia.edu   phone: (212) 854-3774

The publisher gratefully acknowledges the support of
the Forbes Foundation.

First Edition, January 1998

Library of Congress Catalog Number: 97-69356
ISBN 0-9659890-0-3

This collection of poems is released in conjunction with a Website at:
http://www.columbia.edu/cu/ssp/writing/quarto/

LITERATURE & LANGUAGE DEPT.
CHICAGO PUBLIC LIBRARY
400 SOUTH STATE STREET
CHICAGO, IL 60605

"The soul does not like to be without its body.

Because without its body it cannot feel or do anything."

–Leonardo Da Vinci

table of contents

his body was an edible sweetbread 1

fruit 2
tree 3
seedling 4
pumpkin 5
bone 6
cock 7
beekeeper 8
husk 9
calyx 10

like a clicking pulse 13

fence 14
red light 15
caduceus 16
clench 17
clutter 18
tall 19

the deepening fault line 21

jar 22
fissure 23
pottage 24
list 25
shadow 26

a fossil folded in a fetal pose 29

egg 30
vein 31
capaneus 32
onion 33

a solid shape in the darkness 35

grafitti 36
pill 37
shape 38
head 39

from time to time a wet fish would appear 41

lily pad 42
hex 43
wind 44
pulse 45
fisher 46
eating 47

a glowing core 49

pod 50
rivulet 51
hole 52
bauble 53
basin 54

the center source of this velvety inferno 57

wings 58
centipede 59
knitting 60
pangolin 61
bronze 62
mud 63
canary 64–65

credits

Cover photo: Andy Shen

Sculpture on cover: "pellet" by kim white, patinated plaster inscribed with the words, "She regurgitated a bile-soaked pellet. It came to life, sprouting tiny legs and a thick tail, squirming like a wet salamander."

Illustration: kim white from the hieroglyph series.

acknowledgements

I would like to acknowledge the help and encouragement of Alan Ziegler whose counsel during the creation and compilation of this collection was instrumental.

I am grateful to the Forbes Foundation and the Columbia University Creative Writing Center for their help in making this publication possible. And to *The New York Press* where seven of these poems appeared (in slightly different versions) on the back page classified ad section during 1995, as part of an experiment by the author.

Thanks are due to my husband Michael McCaffery for his love and support. And also to Rita Augustine and Nancy Bower for copyediting.

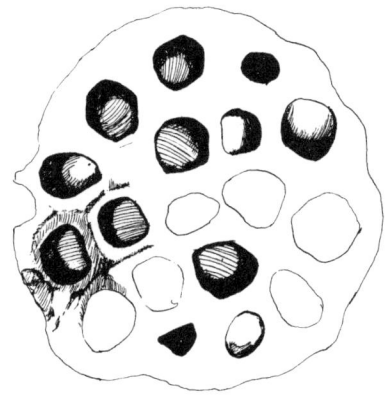

his body was an edible sweetbread

fruit

One day her breasts began to ripen, the darkness of her nipples spread outward until firm flesh transformed into sweet, heavy fruit. The sweetmeats formed all over her chest, soft and purplish cocoa inside thin skin-sacs that hung in clusters from neck to navel. They were not fleshy tumors, they were real fruit, fruit that could be harvested and eaten. Strong-smelling, intoxicating fruit, which intimidated everyone. She was feared and desired, misunderstood and abused. She retreated to a solitary place, and lived out her life in seclusion, feeding off her own mysterious fruit.

tree

There was a man who struggled with a gritty sensation in his stomach. It was not so much painful as it was strange. The skin in that place began to arc up and extend outward, hardening and transforming into woody bark. This outgrowth became so substantial that the man could no longer stand or move about. He was forced to lie on his back and spread his arms to keep from tipping. The tree also grew *inside* his body, slowly taking it, making roots from his veins, transforming his spine into a thick hairy tuber and sending it down into the earth. Finally, the tree covered over all traces of the man. No one looking could see that its sap was bloody red and there was a tiny heart, still pumping inside the concentric rings of its hard wooden torso.

seedling

She had a tiny door in her chest. A thick door made of all the layers of flesh and bone from the surface to the center of her body. Behind this door was a small vaulted chamber which held a single seed that was slowly growing. When she was alone, she would open the door to look inside. The seed sent up a waxy sprout, with a wispy stem and three tiny wrinkled leaves. She watched and worried over the plant, guarding it behind her bones, nourishing it with her blood, using her body as a nursery, a darkened humid hothouse next to her thumping heart.

pumpkin

His pubic hair grew past his ankles. It stiffened and changed into fibrous vegetable vines with pickered velvet leaves. Clusters of yellow flowers became tiny orange tubers, which grew into oversized, fluted bulbous squash. The harvest could not be removed without intense pain, so he dragged the heavy produce everywhere he went, the vines draped over his forearm like a bridal train, pumpkins bumping along on the ground.

bone

There was a smooth, long bone growing up from the center of her gut. It formed deep in her pelvis and stretched up toward her throat: a thickening pointed horn, which showed no signs of halting. She feared its choking fullness as it rose in her throat. She thought it might pierce the skin in the hollow of her neck or rise up from under her tongue and curve out of her mouth.

cock

A row of red phalluses grew on his bald head like a cock's crown. Most of the time they lay flat and rubbery against his skull. But certain times of day, when the sun touched his head, they stood stiffly upright, like an outspread hand, swaying from side to side as he walked.

beekeeper

His body was a cavernous apiary. The internal organs were heaping structures of oozing combs, shuffling with bees. They milked the flowers and made honey in his blood, filling him with soft, fragrant wax. His body was an edible sweetbread. The buzzing swarm coated his head with velvety pollen and covered his face like a shifting hood.

husk

She became dry and hollow, like a husk, a brittle bean sleeve, a dusty drawer. Her contents were emptied and used, scooped out in a single swooping moment. She was open on one side and could not resist being harvested.

calyx

Her scalp began to tingle. The skull softened and started to open. With a painless bursting sensation, her head bloomed. It spread like a folding flower, the liquid around her brain pooling in the cuplike blossom. With the wrinkled organ perched on the stem of her neck like a ripened seed, ready to drop.

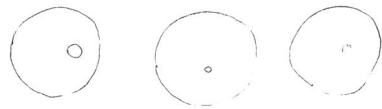

like a clicking pulse

fence

There was a boy who was frightened by almost everything. He crawled in between the fieldstones of an ancient fence. In this tiny gap, he became permanently wedged. He enjoyed the world from this vantage point, safe and invisible. Two blinking eyes in a dark fissure, like a creature peering out from its burrow, except that he never came out. He grew like a bound foot, stunted and immobile, living and dying within the fence.

red light

There is a blinking red light embedded deep in her chest. It keeps her on edge, stretched taut as a rubber band. It is always on, throbbing inside her like a clicking pulse. It emits a siren sound a constant halting scream. As thoughts proceed through her body, they become congested like moths around this angry beacon. Tumbling over one another only to singe themselves.

caduceus

There is a winged silver serpent that circles her head like a satellite. It wraps round her neck or torso and enters her, lodging in her liver like a heavy sinker, hissing in her blood. While she sleeps, it slides through her skin, spreading like mercury on her chest. Coiled, with wings flapping, it transports her into dreams and nightmares.

clench

She would reach frantically into the air and snap something up. Holding it tightly in her hand, she would quickly hide it in her body. She was able to lift her skin and stuff things underneath. Sometimes she was at it all day, hopping and grabbing, scurrying and stuffing. Unseen things were packed into every cavity, clumping into hardening cysts, sticking out everywhere like bumpy pouches.

clutter

The clutter that had been accumulating in her mind began to spill out into her home. Thoughts, memories and worries spewed from her head and condensed in midair as a hail of objects. Everywhere she went she left behind a dribbling trail of tacky trinkets. Her house was stiflingly full, yet she could not dispose of anything. She clung with a strange fondness to the overwhelming clutter.

tall

He was tall in his house. The furniture was removed to make room for his increasing size. Safe in his lair, he grew so large that he had to lift the roof like a box top to leave his house. But when his foot touched down outside the walls, he shrank to the size of a mouse. Scurrying to his office alongside other mini men and woman, who on occasion would see a giant stroll through the crowd. A man who remained large outside his house.

the deepening fault line

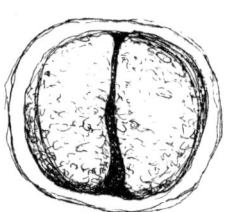

jar

She no longer has a body, she traded it for a clean, cool glass jar, and that is where she lives. She inhabits the jar as a clear and thick, mucusy liquid. This is her essence, all her being condensed into a pungent organic viscose. She sits on a stainless steel shelf, in an experimental laboratory. Scientists are working to reduce her even further, to completely divorce her of any organic ties, to eliminate the embarrassing biological functions of growth and decay. To distill her into a supreme free-floating incarnation.

fissure

In the middle of her life, she began dividing.

Her body developed a cleft-like fissure through its vertical center, and she felt herself shifting, separating.

On one side of the deepening fault line was an expansive body, light and buoyant, with blurred features and undeveloped forms. On the other side was a dense and ever-tightening knot of muscle; a hard, condensed version of herself. As the process accelerated, she had to decide which of these bodies she would inhabit, which one would survive and which one would be left to shrink and fall away. In her indecision, the process halted and would not resume. She was stuck, forever unfinished; a foggy ghost and a weeping red tumor, with a folded groove dividing.

pottage

There was a woman who, during a fit of depression, coughed up her own soul. She held it in her cupped hands for a long time, staring at it. It was heavy and moist, hot and deep purple. She could not bring herself to swallow it. Instead she dropped it into a jar where it landed with a sucking sound. As she screwed the cap on the jar and placed it on a shelf, she began to recognize a distinct difference in her mood, a light, emotionless clarity. Her soul within the jar began to shrink resembling a hard, tiny raisin. As it shrank, she expanded; devoid of the feelings that used to preoccupy her, she felt a kind of vapid freedom. She discarded the jar, deciding to remain like this.

list

He tried to fill his life with a slowly growing list of achievements. He must have believed that when the list was impressive enough, it would speak for itself. It would serve as an unquestioned testimony to his success, and he could rest comfortably behind it like a protecting shield. As his list became substantial, he began being recognized as the man behind the list. This was a relief at first, the easy interaction with strangers, the instant respect from colleagues. But he soon discovered that what was meant to be removable armor had become a permanent shell. Thickening as its contents slowly disappeared.

shadow

She could see her life in front of her, somehow it stood outside her and was visible to her. Its distinctive silhouette could be seen clearly, moving in a peculiar, determined way and she would simply follow its lead.
It was a comforting phantom, like a shadow, only it was cast with no light and moved independently of its source. Actually, she was its shadow, she was the shadow of her own life. It walked ahead of her, flowing along the ground, dragging her behind by her toes.

a fossil folded in a fetal pose

egg

He came from a cold white egg. Curled in the center like a fossil folded in a fetal pose. He emerged long after the shell had crumbled and fallen away. With a hesitating shiver, he slid through a tear in the thick, rubbery membrane. Born as a fully grown man, but without desire. With the eerie vacuousness of a backward sage, retreating from life before it's known. He moved in the outside world like someone awakening from a dreamless sleep, stiff and mute; cold as death and unable to generate his own heat.

vein

She had a single, tiny vein, thin as a thread. It roamed beneath the surface of her powdery pale, pink skin. The vein could be seen curling through her body like a delicate red line. It wound round her purple organs and attached itself to her tiny heart. Her muscles were silky thin for lack of nourishment. She lay reclining on her couch, with scarcely the strength to breathe. She had no arteries or branching veins, only this single capillary upon which she fiercely depended. This tender vein which carried the lifeblood to her fragile wilting body, one cell at a time.

capaneus

A man lived in the scorched cavity of a dormant volcano.
In the violent heat of the afternoon, he would sleep,
half-buried in the charred ash. At night, he would wander
the sterile landscape of the caldera floor. His feet were
scarred from the burning sand. His thick and scaly skin
hung on his bones like a rumpled sock. When he breathed,
his ribs could be seen working, rising and falling. His face,
lips and eyelids were hard and cracked, speckled with
brown ashen tones, and he was always thirsty.
At daybreak, he would crawl slowly up the volcano's wall,
sit on the rim and stare into the desolate gouge,
the parched, fiery abyss which was invented for him.

sour

She always smelt pungent. She had a sharp and distinctive odor which was, at times, quite unflattering. She was hard and sour, and as she became older she began to soften and rot. Soon people could tell just by looking at her how vulnerable she was, they could poke and squeeze her and there was nothing she could do. Her skin became excessively dry and transparent, it fell off in crisp, scaly layers. In this way she began to lose control, the outside of herself slowly falling away, while the inside turned soft and black.

a solid shape in the darkness

grafitti

A map was tattooing itself to the inside of her skull. Burning, pricking needles were at work within that dark, electrified moat between the brain and its seawall. This strange map manifested itself as a sharp, throbbing pressure, a tangle of pain and purpose, and her mind squinted to make out its shapes. It was completely accurate, this map, an outline of who she was, of her fortune and fate. But when the pain subsided, the map could not be seen. Etched on the backside of her eyes, illuminated only in the process of its making.

pill

It was some kind of medicine. Shaped like a bean, bright and candy-coated, hard as a tiny stone. She held it in her mouth, rolling it around with her tongue. It was sweet at first, then bitter. When she swallowed it, it left a trail of crackling fizz all the way down to her stomach, where it settled like sand into a soft crevasse on the floor of the wrinkled sac. The harsh acids seemed to have no effect on the bright pill, and it was never flushed into the lower intestine. It remained in the stomach, and became as active as a jumping bean, ricocheting against the rumbling stomach walls, uncorroded, undissolved and useless.

shape

He held an image of her in his mind. A continuous screenplay of every way he could remember seeing her, every stance and gesture, her line and form. While he viewed this moving memory, another image floated unseeable behind the illuminated passion play. A solid shape in the darkness, below his conscious thoughts, a shape with weight, but fragile as a fingerprint. Something he knew would tell him everything about her.

head

There was a man who could take off his head and walk around with it tucked under his arm. His sensory perceptions seeped in through his skin, he made decisions with his bowels and spoke through his navel. He could shuttle between two worlds as easily as putting on a hat, and thought nothing of his facility. Enjoying life like a completed man.

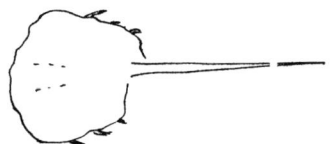

from time to time a wet fish would appear

lily pad

The man saw that there was the bud of a flower growing in the palm of his hand. It was firm and pink, and when it opened there was a shy, tiny face inside. The face never spoke or smiled, it simply stared in an odd, quizzical way. The man did not know anything about the face, but he felt tenderly towards it and carefully protected it. He never used the hand that belonged to the flowerface; he held it at his side in a loose fist, so that no one could see. At night he would open his hand and lay it palm up, beside his cheek. As he fell asleep the face would begin to hum. It hummed softly all night, and the man would experience the most moving, astonishing dreams.

hex

The sun came into her bedroom, filling it almost completely, and there was little room for anything else. She crawled into the room on hands and knees and slid underneath the sun. Into the small space between floor, wall and heavy-hung sphere, lying on her side with warm golden liquid globe resting heavily on her shoulder, sinking into the valley between iliac crest and seventh rib, she was reclining, golden Atlas in the heat of the pale ochre light.

wind

She was invisible. She evaporated in the womb and was born without her mother knowing. She had no mass, no hungry body. She was a silent ghost tiptoeing along the surface of the earth, listening to every whispered hope and fear. She could see thoughts and memories as though they were solid objects, she collected them but had none of her own. She could slide in and out of the bodies of others, and they would be aware, suddenly, of all the things she knew.

pulse

There was a blind woman who could feel the pulse in stone. Cool sharp rock with water flowing over it, or a smooth stone buried in a pathway. She knew them upon contact, knew their ancient histories. She understood the palisades, jagged mountains and ringed craters, as a physician understands the body, and she knew the shifting moods of the lava flowing beneath. She was a kind of osteopath, who could set the bones of the earth, reshaping them, like the wind or the relentless sea.

fisher

There was a woman who lived in a big city, dressed like a fisherman, and went around with a net and bucket. She never left the city, but her skin had a ruddy glow, as though touched by the sun and salty wind. She would fish in open public spaces; sidewalks and lobbies, sitting patient and still with her net poised, staring at a spot on the floor. Once in a while she would scoop her net, clicking the rim loudly on the dry pavement. Onlookers would shake their heads or laugh out loud. But, from time to time, a wet fish would appear flipping and struggling in the net. She would dump it into her bucket, where it would swim quietly in a circle. People were amazed at first, but quickly decided that it was some kind of trick, that she was just a street performer, and they would toss a coin thoughtlessly into her bucket.

eating

She took him apart with tweezers. Tweezers which emerged from the tip of her rich, wet tongue. Smooth, sharp ivory pincers, so tiny she could lift off a few cells at a time, eating them like snowflakes. This was the strange way she consumed him, effecting a slow erosion, while stroking him with her skillful tongue. For years it continued like this. She would take parts of him. He would ignore the relentless pinching pain, and not acknowledge his own slow dissolution. Finally and abruptly, she buried her face in his armpit, burrowed into his chest and plucked out his soul. She held it for a moment, soft and quivering on the tip of her tongue, then swallowed it whole. It slid down her throat like a slick, sweet bean.

a glowing core

pod

He built for himself a mummy's cell. A crusty cocoon made with a clear, waxy resin that oozed from the tip of his thick pink tongue. Starting at his toes, he encased himself, dabbing the edge of the shell with his mouth as though eating in reverse. Soon he was entirely concealed, entombed in the pod like a bundled traveler, silent and alone.

rivulet

She had been resting peacefully in the side of a mountain. Frozen in a block of bluish-green ice. Her skin had frosted over, reflecting light like a transparent rhinestone. For thousands of years she lived like this, vibrating in every crystallized cell, a spirit creature in a whitened larval corpse. When they discovered her, they chipped her out of the ice and carried her down the mountain. Laid out on a stainless steel table, they began to cut her open and pick her apart. But, when they reached into the body, the internal organs instantly collapsed. Under the light of the examining table, her body quickly melted. Sliding down a drain in the center of the table like a clear glacial rivulet.

hole

She was burning. From the center out, a hole was

growing larger. There were no red flames, no hissing fire,

only a silent, widening circle, crisp, and charred

at the edges. Where her navel had been, there was a

deepening depression, wet and purple, like a sinking sore.

She could see inside. She could see her coiled bowels

slowly unraveling, curling around a glowing core

like a twisting snake, furling out through the hole

as a thin ribbon of smoke.

bauble

She fell into the ocean and was swallowed up by the waves. Floating there in the briny stomach of the sea as an alien, a stranger, an irritant. Her skin began to form a shell which built upon itself. Layer after glowing layer. Until she was completely encased in a hardened, milky orb. She rolled along the bottom and came to rest in the coldest, darkest cavern, like a blind, sunken eye. Like a single perfect thought that remains unknown.

basin

There was a woman who became a basin. Her reclining body curled and spread, limbs merging into the hollowed mass of her changing shape. Her smooth skin became polished marble, and all her features were lost except for her navel, out of which somehow bubbled a sweet-tasting water which filled her new form.

the center source of this velvety inferno

wings

She had been born with wings, huge magnificent dragonfly wings, twelve feet in span. Reflective, iridescent wings that made a thunderous, buzzing sound. She would fly with her mouth open and lips distended, gulping up songbirds and frightened sparrows. People gathered to watch for her, but rarely saw her. When she did appear, she came, startlingly, from nowhere, fast and ferocious. Her face was like lightning, so bright they had to put their hands over their eyes and fall to the ground to avoid being hit.

centipede

She had hundreds of tiny legs that she kept concealed under her clothes, and fine antennae tied back into her hair. At night she would unfurl her silky feelers and massage the air with her rippling rows of legs. Her body was segmented and she could move along the walls like a crustaceous snake. During the day she gave all appearances of being a normal woman and nobody knew her secret, careful as she was to reveal herself only when alone and in the dark.

knitting

There was a man who had hands for feet. He wore mittens

for socks and walked with a skittering sideways step.

During the day he collected material, strands of thread,

rope and hair; things he could twist into a kind of yarn.

The evenings he spent knitting with his four arms,

moving like a monkey in a frantic game of cat's cradle.

His work filled every room, strung from corner to corner.

He would lie in them even as he worked, swinging softly

like a quiet spider in a woven web.

pangolin

He had delicate, spiny skin that sometimes appeared as scales, sometimes as feathers. His house was built into the side of a cliff at the edge of an ocean. In the evening he dove into the white-capped water, emerging again the following morning. On rare occasions, he would stay below for several days. During these times tensions ran high on shore. The people watched and waited on the palisades, knowing how much depended on the sight of him rising, unharmed.

bronze

A deep incision was made in his leg, but instead of blood, a thick, oily, white fluid seeped out. When they folded back the skin to reach his broken bone, they found it made of hollow bronze, filled with steaming molten marrow and glowing like a filament. Never had anyone seen metal like this, living in a man's body, as a man's bones. They welded his bone back together. He was fixed in this way, as a machine is fixed. After the weld had cooled and the wound was stitched, he could have walked home. But they elected to wrap his leg in a plaster cast. To let him go about with crutches as though he had within him brittle human cartilage and common, syrupy red marrow.

mud

There was a child who had been formed entirely from mud. He lived alone in a fertile forest and smelled of its dampness. No one raised him and his creator was unknown. Moreover, he never aged or grew into an adult. He scampered and played in the forest without changing.

canary

The child was exceedingly beautiful, more like light than matter. When you looked at him, it seemed your eyes could not focus. He moved about in a sulfurous, glowing haze. With soft, buoyant golden hair that seemed to flutter around his head like a feathery crown. He had an unusual, compelling scent. It was like the freshness of youth and you could detect it from a great distance. He was perfect and lovely except for his sadly misshapen face. His teeth grew straight out of his mouth like a horny bill and he had no lips. He had never spoken a word to anyone, and there was something so disturbing in his nervous stare, that no one dared approach him.

He lived alone in the secret hollows of an abandoned mine. Rarely seen, but often heard, he would stand rigidly on pointed toes, intense and hysterical, singing in the stone tunnels. The songs had no words, they were a rhythmic, melodic pain-cry. Piercingly shrill, frighteningly yellow songs that resonated along the hollow corridors and seeped up through the earth.

The child died alone, somewhere in that darkened maze. He caught fire and was consumed in an extraordinary, silent blaze. The flames extended slowly in all directions curling out as a creeping yellow vapor, hovering around the child like a thick, floating fog. He stood as the center source of this velvety inferno. His dark, whiteless eyes were wide open as his beaky mouth issued a new version of his song. It resonated with such shrill intensity that the stone above him broke, and light streamed into his self-appointed tomb.